MW01201696

be calm.
A GUIDED JOURNAL

be calm.

A GUIDED JOURNAL

prompts and practices to
RELIEVE ANXIETY

Christopher Hutcheson, LCSW

**ROCKRIDGE
PRESS**

To my muses three:
my beautiful wife, Jennifer,
and two lovely daughters, Madeline and Audrey.

Copyright © 2021 by Rockridge Press, Emeryville, California

No part of this publication may be reproduced, stored in a retrieval system, or transmitted in any form or by any means, electronic, mechanical, photocopying, recording, scanning, or otherwise, except as permitted under Sections 107 or 108 of the 1976 United States Copyright Act, without the prior written permission of the Publisher. Requests to the Publisher for permission should be addressed to the Permissions Department, Rockridge Press, 6005 Shellmound Street, Suite 175, Emeryville, CA 94608.

Limit of Liability/Disclaimer of Warranty: The Publisher and the author make no representations or warranties with respect to the accuracy or completeness of the contents of this work and specifi-cally disclaim all warranties, including without limitation warranties of fitness for a particular purpose. No warranty may be created or extended by sales or promotional materials. The advice and strategies contained herein may not be suitable for every situation. This work is sold with the understanding that the Publisher is not engaged in rendering medical, legal, or other professional advice or services. If professional assistance is required, the services of a competent professional person should be sought. Neither the Pub-lisher nor the author shall be liable for damages arising herefrom. The fact that an individual, organization, or website is referred to in this work as a citation and/or potential source of further informa-tion does not mean that the author or the Publisher endorses the information the individual, organization, or website may provide or recommendations they/it may make. Further, readers should be aware that websites listed in this work may have changed or disap-peared between when this work was written and when it is read.

For general information on our other products and services or to obtain technical support, please contact our Customer Care Department within the United States at (866) 744-2665, or outside the United States at (510) 253-0500.

Rockridge Press publishes its books in a variety of electronic and print formats. Some content that appears in print may not be available in electronic books, and vice versa.

TRADEMARKS: Rockridge Press and the Rockridge Press logo are trademarks or registered trademarks of Callisto Media Inc. and/or its affiliates, in the United States and other countries, and may not be used without written permission. All other trademarks are the property of their respective owners. Rockridge Press is not associ-ated with any product or vendor mentioned in this book.

Interior and Cover Designer: Jill Lee
Art Producer: Samantha Ulban
Editor: Adrian Potts
Production Editor: Andrew Yackira
Production Manager: Martin Worthington

All images used under license Shutterstock.

Author Photo Courtesy of Christina Wagner (clynnphotoanddesign.com).

ISBN: Print 978-1-63807-011-5

R0

Contents

Introduction

I'm so glad our paths have crossed. As a licensed clinical social worker (LCSW), I specialize in the treatment of depression and anxiety using talk therapy. My practice, Gentle Beacon, is located in Lafayette, Indiana. Over the past 13 years, I've had the privilege of working with hundreds of people, of all ages, colors, religions, ethnicities, and genders, from all over the world. In a variety of ways, their anxious thoughts, feelings, and behaviors were stopping them from living their lives to the fullest. What I've learned from working with them is that recovering from anxiety is not only possible but probable.

If anxiety has stopped you from living your fullest life, this journal is for you. It takes the lessons, experience, and research I've gathered and puts it all into useful, actionable, and personalized strategies you can use to remedy the worrying, tense, and exhausting feeling of chronic anxiety. That said, this journal is not a replacement for mental health treatment by a licensed professional. See the resources on page 173 for assistance.

Why We Suffer from Anxiety

Imagine that it's 10,000 years ago, and while you are out searching for food, you suddenly encounter a tiger on the prowl. You immediately feel anxious because your body is instinctively preparing you to either flee the situation or fight for your life. Every ounce of focus you have is on that tiger, and rightly so.

This fight-or-flight response exists to keep us alive or at least out of harm's way. These days, though, you don't run across tigers while searching the aisles in the grocery store. Still, you may feel anxious because you are perceiving some sort of danger or harm. If there's a reason for it—such as an angry shopper threatening to ram their cart into yours because you are blocking an aisle—anxiety is natural and can even be helpful, alerting you to get out of the way. In this way, anxiety can be *adaptive*; it alerts you to take action. However, when there's no apparent cause of the anxiety (that is, there is no in-the-moment risk), anxiety can be *maladaptive*, interfering with your life and how you function.

Fortunately, with tools and strategies to relieve anxiety, you can and will get better. Your brain will grow and change over time as the result of your new experiences.

How to Use This Book

This book is an interactive journal. It is meant for you to write, scribble, and draw in. The prompts and exercises are based on acceptance and commitment therapy (ACT), mindfulness practice, and cognitive behavioral therapy (CBT); these are all evidence-based tools and strategies to assist you on your journey. In other words, research has proven their effectiveness.

The general idea is that if we change our thoughts about an experience (a feeling, a thought, or a behavior), we can change how we feel about it—and vice versa. Imagine a triangle with feelings in one corner, behavior in another, and thoughts in the third. These represent the three main paths to change, which lead to relief from a wide range of anxiety symptoms.

This journal is divided into these three main sections, too. A change in one corner of the triangle will affect the other two. If you change your feelings—like learning strategies to calm your fear and anxiety in social situations—then you will likely change your thoughts ("When I calm my anxiety, I can contribute to the conversation and connect with others") and your behavior (you stop avoiding social activities). Simply put, if you're trying to effect change, you can start with any corner of the triangle.

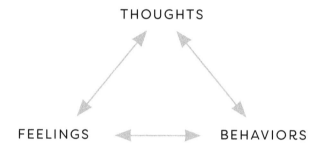

If You're Looking to Address Specific Symptoms . . .

You don't have to use this journal from front to back. If you need help with a particular challenge, skip to the section you need:

- If you're consumed by worried or intrusive thinking, start with section three, Thoughts (page 88).

- If your anxiety is causing you to avoid important people, places, and/or events, start with section two, Behavior (page 46).

- If you're struggling with your feelings or physical side effects of anxiety, start with section one, Feelings (page x).

If You're Looking to Manage Your Anxiety in General . . .

If you have difficulty in all parts of the thoughts-feelings-behavior triangle or just feel anxious in general, you might want to work through this journal page by page. You don't need to complete large chunks in one go; in fact, try not to move through the journal too quickly. For instance, you might respond to a single journal prompt and then think about it for a few minutes, hours, or even days. Also, when completing an exercise, give yourself time to think about it and then practice it. Just like anything you endeavor to do, practicing these strategies will increase your skills. Give yourself a chance to succeed.

Using This Journal as a Companion to *Be Calm*

Although this journal can be used on its own, it can also be used as a companion to *Be Calm: Proven Techniques to Stop Anxiety Now*. The sections in this journal correspond to the sections in that book. So, as you are working on the prompts and exercises in this journal, you may want to read the corresponding section in *Be Calm* for more support. It is based on the same evidence-based tools as this journal: CBT, ACT, and mindfulness practice. But, as mentioned, you can work with just this journal and still achieve maximum benefit.

SECTION

I

feelings

Feelings do not define you. Rather, you have feelings in response to an experience. Some experiences create good feelings, and others uncomfortable ones. Whatever they are, feelings need to be expressed because suppressing them can make anxiety worse. The more you avoid feelings such as sadness, fear, and anger, the more anxious you'll likely feel.

The prompts, affirmations, and exercises here can help you learn to identify, express, and accept difficult emotions. First, we'll look at "Processing Your Emotions," where you'll do some reflection, journaling, and practice around strong emotions. Then we'll move on to "Boosting Body Awareness" to explore and learn to accept sensations associated with strong feelings.

Processing Your Emotions

"As long as you keep secrets and suppress information, you are fundamentally at war with yourself... The critical issue is allowing yourself to know what you know. That takes an enormous amount of courage."

—Bessel van der Kolk

Our emotions allow us to make connections with other people, help us make decisions, and motivate us into action. However, when we feel overwhelmed by our emotions, it can become difficult to process them, and we may push them away or avoid them. Over time, this can actually reinforce anxious thoughts and anxiety-driven behaviors. Learning to better identify and address your emotions will allow you to gain greater emotional control and help you feel better.

When you were growing up, how did the adults in your home show their emotions? If you showed *your* emotions, how did they respond to you? Did your family have unspoken rules about how to express feelings or when it was appropriate to show them (if ever)? How might this have influenced how you express and feel about your emotions today?

Write about a time during your childhood or adolescence when you had a strong feeling of anxiety or another uncomfortable feeling. As you write, think like a reporter, covering the facts of where, when, who, and what.

Looking back at the previous prompt, what, if anything, did you do to cope with those feelings? Was your coping method successful? If not, consider if part of the problem is not allowing yourself to reflect on and accept deeper emotional experiences. As you respond, show yourself self-compassion and self-acceptance. Tell yourself, "It's okay to feel (*name the emotion*)."

Have you ever used a substance such as alcohol, cannabis, or nicotine to cope with strong emotions? If so, how did it help? If you still use this substance regularly, does the cost outweigh the benefit? If so, how do you feel about seeking guidance from a mental health professional or a 12-step program, online or in your area?

"I said: What about my heart?

He said: Tell me what you hold inside it?

I said: Pain and sorrow.

He said: Stay with it. The wound is the place where the Light enters you."

—Unknown

MINDFUL GROUNDING

Grounding yourself in the moment can help you gain clarity around what you are feeling. This mindfulness exercise engages all five of your senses, giving you some distance from your emotions to provide hints on how to respond to what's happening, whether that's using a technique to address your anxiety or expressing what you are feeling.

1. Find a comfortable position, and take a few deep breaths until you feel yourself settling in. Then, focus on your breathing. Gently shift your focus to each of your senses, as follows.

2. Focus on your sense of sight. Attend to your physical surroundings by making a mental note of the colors and shapes you see. What type of space are you in?

3. Focus on your sense of hearing. Pay close attention, making a mental note of everything you can hear.

4. Focus on your sense of smell. What can you smell, if anything?

5. Focus on your sense of touch. Can you feel your clothes? Can you feel the ground, chair, or bed beneath you?

6. Shift your focus to your sense of taste. Can you taste anything?

7. Shift your focus back to your breathing. How do you feel now?

I define myself. I am strong. I am resilient.
I am taking action to change my life.
I do what works for me

All humans sometimes experience uncomfortable feelings like anger, shame, sadness, help-lessness, or fear. Make a list of the top three feelings you find uncomfortable or that cause you anxiety. What is it about those feelings that you find so uncomfortable?

Knowing what triggers your feelings can provide important insight. Refer to the previous prompt, and think about a time you felt one of your top three uncomfortable feelings. On a scale of 1 to 10 (with 1 being very mildly uncomfortable and 10 being the most uncomfortable you have ever felt), how intense was the feeling? What was going on at the time?

DISTRESS SCALE

You can use the Subjective Units of Distress Scale (SUDS) to practice noticing how distressing an experience is on a scale from 1 to 10 (with 1 being the least distress possible and 10 the most distress you've ever felt). It can be helpful to track this over time; try it now and keep further records.

Think back to the most recent situation that caused you anxiety and envision the details of the situation. Note what was happening around you.

1. Note what you were thinking. (This is usually a phrase.)

2. Note what you were feeling.

3. How intense was this feeling on the SUDS scale?

After using SUDs each day over the span of a week or longer, you will have collected enough data to draw some conclusions. Are these experiences similar or dissimilar in certain ways? Similarities may indicate that your anxiety has a common cause, and differences suggest that maybe your anxiety has more than one cause.

The brain loves to predict the outcome of an event—even though it can't know the future. Think of a recent situation you were about to experience that caused you to feel a certain way. What did your brain predict would happen? Did it actually end that way? How did you feel afterward?

When we judge ourselves or imagine that others are judging us, it can create immense suffering or, at the very least, uncomfortable feelings. What would your life be like if you worried less about mistakes, made fewer judgments, and forgave yourself? Write yourself a note, showing yourself compassion and letting yourself know that you accept yourself just as you are.

When you're feeling strong emotions, finding a way to express those feelings can go a long way toward helping you process them. The act of talking, labeling, and expressing emotions helps you better understand yourself and feel more in control of your emotions. Write down the names of up to three people you can think of to open up to this week, and jot down their contact information. It may be people you know—or perhaps you might reach out to a therapist or find a support group online.

Now, write down the things you would find helpful to talk about. When you're ready, reach out to at least one of these people or groups. Remember, there's no shame in acknowledging your anxiety. In fact, talking about it can help you feel more accepted and less anxious.

S.T.O.P.

A feeling can start and rapidly grow in an instant and, before you know it, you may be reacting in a way that you wish you hadn't. The S.T.O.P. strategy can interrupt this snowball effect by allowing you to acknowledge the feeling and then decide how you want to respond. So, the next time you feel overwhelmed by anxious feelings, remember this acronym:

Stop. Literally stop what you are doing entirely.

Take a few deep breaths to center yourself and bring yourself into the present moment.

Observe what's really going on. Are you really in the danger that anxiety is trying to show you?

Proceed with what works. This means taking into account what is happening in *this exact moment*, and taking the action that makes the most sense for you. This could be taking more time to breathe, changing your focus of the situation, or reaching out to a trusted friend.

The only person experiencing your feelings is you. Even when the feeling is powerful, sometimes it's best to let it pass rather than try to solve it or talk yourself out of it. Has there been a time when trying to fight off or "solve" the feeling only heightened it? What do you think would happen if you accepted your feelings for what they are in the moment and just allowed them to come and go?

What I am experiencing now will be less powerful in the next seconds, minutes, hours, and days of my life. I cannot feel the same way forever.

DEEP BREATHING

Deep breathing has the ability to change our blood chemistry and stimulate relaxation. The cool thing about breathing is that you don't need any equipment. Deep breathing gives you the fuel, time, and opportunity to reduce physical symptoms of anxiety in your body and reenergizes you to move forward.

1. Make a note of how anxious you feel on a scale of 1 to 10 (see page 13).

2. Find a comfortable spot, and set a gentle timer for five minutes.

3. Slowly breathe in through your nose for three or more seconds, allowing your breath to fill your belly. At the top of the breath, pause for a moment (less than a second).

4. Release the breath through your nose for at least three or more seconds.

5. Repeat this in-and-out breath until the timer goes off.

6. How anxious do you feel now on the scale? Hopefully, it is a lower number. If you'd like to decrease it further, repeat the steps for another five minutes.

Boosting Body Awareness

"To experience embodied awareness, take notice of the underlying sensations that actually inform you about how you feel."

—Peter Levine and
Maggie Phillips

Because anxiety is part of the body's stress system, it often shows up as physical symptoms, such as tenseness in the chest, shortness of breath, or a temperature change in part of the body. These physical sensations can then influence your emotional state and exacerbate your anxiety. Recognizing, naming, and acknowledging these sensations boosts your awareness of your body and gives you tools to take care of your physical health and deal with symptoms when they arise.

Sleep is important to your ability to cope with anxiety. Being more aware of your relationship with sleep can help you identify ways to improve your sleeping habits (see the exercise on the next page for guidance). Write about your sleeping habits here:

How are you sleeping these days?

How many hours do you usually get? Does it feel like a good amount?

Are you able to fall asleep easily? If not, why?

How many times do you usually wake up during the night? How long does it usually take you to fall back sleep?

On a scale of 1 to 10, how rested do you usually feel when you wake up?

THE SLEEP SCHEDULE

Getting a good night's sleep can boost your mood levels throughout the day and help you manage your anxiety. Sometimes, doing the same thing each evening for two weeks before going to bed can help prepare the body for entering its resting period and establish healthy sleeping habits. The first step is to turn off all screens (yes, this includes phones, tablets, laptops, and televisions) two hours before you lie down to sleep. The rest is up to you. In this two-hour window, try to do the exact same things every evening. For example, after you shut off all screens, perhaps you:

- 1 hour 50 minutes before bed: Read

- 1 hour before bed: Take a shower

- 30 minutes before bed: Brew and have some caffeine-free tea

- 5 minutes before bed: Practice deep breathing (see page 22)

Write down your own presleep routine and try it out for two weeks. Notice what benefits emerge.

- 2 hours before: shut off screens

Take a moment to check in with your body. Are you noticing sensations you aren't ordinarily aware of? If you have chronic stress, chances are you aren't as in touch with your body as you could be. What are your top stressors? How do they affect your functioning? What simple changes could you make to care for your body amid the stress?

SUBTLE SMILE

Smiling even if you don't feel like it can "trick" your brain into noticing your expression and feeling better about what is going on. Try this out now, and again the next time you feel anxious. Because the smile is subtle (sneaky, almost), you can practice this even among people.

1. Notice your facial expression. Are you frowning? Are you tense? Are your eyes narrowed or squinting at all? Maybe your expression is blank right now.

2. Slowly release the tension in your forehead if you noticed some. Allow it to unfurrow.

3. Relax the muscles around your eyes. Allow them to be soft and aware.

4. Relax your cheeks and chin muscles.

5. Slowly draw up the corners of your mouth into a subtle smile and hold it for a moment.

6. If you're alone, or if it makes sense to do so in a group, say, "Hello." Your greeting will sound cheerier than it otherwise might because the simple act of smiling tricks the brain's neural networks into thinking that everything is good.

Using substances such as alcohol, cannabis, nicotine, and even caffeine can have a negative effect on your body and thus on your emotions and stress levels. If you've used them, how do each of these substances affect you? For example, some may relax you, and others may be energizing. What are you trying to change about your body when you use them? Do you struggle with any of these substances? How do you feel about contacting a mental health professional or a 12-step program for help?

Even though it seems to take place only in the brain, excessive worrying can be physically exhausting. Write about a time when worrying about a situation affected your ability to physically respond to it the way you would have wanted. How would you do things differently in the future?

BODY SCAN

The body scan exercise can help you tune in to your body. When you know in which part of your body you feel anxiety, you will be better equipped to address it. As you do the scan, stay present in the experience and practice accepting any sensations you notice.

1. Sit or lie comfortably, close your eyes, and take a deep breath.

2. Mindfully and deliberately shift your focus toward your head. Is it holding any tension or discomfort? If so, focus your attention on it, breathe into it, and imagine the tension or discomfort leaving your body through your breath.

3. Repeat step 2 for each body part, all the way down to your toes.

Do your muscles tense up when you feel anxious? If so, which parts of your body get tense? How tense do they get? How aware of this tension are you typically? What do you do to relieve the tension?

"You can't stop the waves, but you can learn to surf."

—Jon Kabat-Zinn

Sometimes it can be difficult to label or describe anxiety. How does your body react or move when you are feeling anxious? If your anxiety had substance, like rock or mist, what form would it take? How would the weight of that substance affect your body?

Restlessness can be a symptoms of anxiety, making it difficult to stay in one place and maintain focus. What was happening around you the last time you felt restless? Describe how it felt and how the restlessness eventually resolved itself. What action did you take, if any?

I am a human. No matter how I feel in any given moment, I am neither better nor worse than anyone else.

SING IT!

Like deep breathing, singing aloud is a great way to stimulate the part of the nervous system that calms and relaxes you. When you are experiencing physical symptoms of anxiety, give it a try. The more often you stimulate this part of your nervous system, the more relaxed you'll feel.

1. Choose a song with words and music you love.

2. Set aside five minutes, or the length of your song, to sing.

3. Find a place to sing where you won't feel self-conscious, such as your bedroom or maybe the shower.

4. When you're ready, play the song and sing along. When the song ends, notice how your body feels.

When you'd rather not notice what's going on because it causes you to feel anxious, being mindful of the present moment might be the last thing you want to do. Write about a situation when time seemed to pass more quickly or more slowly than you would have liked. What might you do in the future to ground yourself in the "moment" for a richer experience?

Our bodies are designed to move, whether that's around the block or up a flight of stairs. How many hours a day are you stationary? How many hours a day do you move around and/or exercise? How does a lack of movement affect your body? How about activity? What effect do they each have on your mood?

_____

_____

_____

_____

_____

_____

_____

_____

_____

_____

_____

_____

Engaging in physical activity can ground you in your body and activate parts of the brain that help relieve anxiety. How do you normally feel after physical activity? Which exercises boost your mood? Maybe it's walking your dog or dancing around your living room. When will you do this next? Schedule it in.

Tuning in to your sense of touch can ground you in the moment and help calm you when anxiety's physical symptoms start to feel overwhelming. Which textures do you enjoy touching? Why do you like about them? Can you carry something with this texture in your pocket and touch it when you need to relax on the go?

THE COST OF HOLDING ON

Toting around unprocessed, heavy emotions like shame, guilt, or anger can sap the body of its physical energy. This exercise helps you experience how this might feel if your emotions were an object you could set down.

1. Find an object with some weight to it such as a book, water bottle, or dumbbell.

2. Take a deep breath and notice how your body feels, from your head to your toes, *before* picking up the object.

3. Slowly and carefully pick up the object. Hold it until you feel some fatigue.

4. Before you put down the load, notice again how your body feels.

5. Put down the load, and notice the relief and restoration you feel upon dropping the weight.

How did your body change as you held on to the burden longer? How about right before putting it down? How might strong feelings that cause a burden also be causing your body discomfort?

I am not my thoughts, feelings, or sensations.
I am _____.

(your name)

I am separate from my thoughts, feelings, and sensations.

SECTION

II

behavior

Anxiety generally results in two main behavior patterns: avoidance and escape. In the case of real danger, running away makes sense. But when your life is not at risk, avoiding or escaping your triggers can limit your experiences in life. Although it might feel good in the moment to get away or avoid certain situations, these patterns may actually increase anxiety over time.

In "Avoiding Avoidance," you'll explore ways your anxiety tricks you into thinking you must flee from or avoid triggers through journal prompts and exercises. Then, in "Accepting Anxiety," you'll start seeing your anxiety from a nonjudgmental perspective and, in this way, perhaps learn to accept it.

Avoiding Avoidance

"Yesterday I was clever and tried to change the world. Today, I am wise, so I am changing myself."

—Unknown

Although it is natural to avoid things that can cause us harm, the anxiety triggers that result in avoidance patterns generally don't pose an actual threat. It's critical to know how avoidance behaviors are affecting your life so that you can learn to approach the discomfort and increase your tolerance for uncertainty. This can help stop your avoidance behaviors from escalating as well as reduce them so that you can live a fuller life.

Avoiding situations or feelings that make you feel bad may provide temporary relief, but because you are not addressing your problems, this can lead to even more avoidance. Over time, this avoidance loop can become an unconscious habit. Take a moment to reflect on your patterns of avoidance. What do you avoid that only causes you problems in the long run? Here are some clues that suggest you're avoiding something that matters or has meaning to you:

- Saying you will do something but then not following through.

- Procrastination: delaying a task until tomorrow . . . then the next day . . . and the next.

- Making rationalizations, justifications, and excuses for why you can't do something. ("My alarm clock didn't wake me up.")

- Wasting energy/time on trivial thoughts, tasks, and interactions as a way to distract yourself from what you should or need to be doing.

- Frequently telling others, or yourself, that you don't feel well physically and that's why you can't do something.

Reacting to anxiety with avoidance can be a natural response to unwanted emotions and doesn't mean you're weak or "bad." It is, however, an unhealthy reaction that negatively impacts your life. Describe how you feel emotionally when you have the urge to react with avoidance.

Internal cues such as nausea, shaking, sweating, or a racing heart might convince you that you *must* stay away from something to stay safe. When you want to avoid something, what internal cues urge you to do so? What danger are you facing, if any? If you go through with it despite those cues, what might happen?

CHOOSE YOUR RHYTHM

Sometimes simply being aware of the body is enough to change it. This includes the basics such as your heartbeat. Whenever you want to find some calm, take a deep breath and try the following:

1. To find your pulse, place the index and middle fingers of your dominant hand on the upturned wrist of your other hand, below your thumb.

2. Once you feel your pulse, mindfully observe the rhythm of your heartbeat. No counting.

3. Over the next few minutes, imagine that the beat is getting slower. There's nothing to prove, so just imagine it.

4. After a few minutes, check in with your body. How do you feel?

What is happening inside of me and outside of me are completely different experiences. The outside doesn't know what is happening inside me unless I tell someone about it.

What situations or scenarios do you avoid to make yourself feel better? What are the benefits of avoiding those things? What are the downsides? Choose one thing you tend to avoid and describe the best-case and worst-case scenario of what could happen if you faced it despite your anxiety.

Because the brain wants to keep the body safe, it might associate something innocuous with something dangerous because these things seem similar. A group of people running toward you could be perceived as threatening, but not if you're standing at the finish line of a race. Sometimes the brain links things like this together. Can you think of ordinary situations your brain might be perceiving as dangerous because of faulty associations? List as many as you can think of.

"Avoiding danger is no safer in the long run than outright exposure. The fearful are caught as often as the bold."

—Helen Keller

Sometimes, the brain senses that we are in real danger and may trigger the preprogrammed fight-or-flight response. Have you been in a situation where you needed to run from danger or stand and fight to protect yourself? What sensations did you feel in your body? What did you do? If faced with a similar situation in the future, what might you do instead, if anything?

If the fight-or-flight response fails, you might freeze or go limp. This is sometimes called "tonic immobility" (aka playing dead). Though it may not look like you are actively avoiding or escaping a situation, you are still checking out. Have you ever found yourself immobilized by your anxiety? If you are familiar with this, describe a time in your life when this happened. How would things have been different if you had taken action? How might you take action in the future if all your senses want you to freeze on the spot?

We are social animals, which can make anxiety in social situations especially difficult to face. Imagine that you are at a gathering and you are feeling anxious. Rather than retreating to a faraway corner or not going to the gathering at all, what are three questions you can ask someone new? What are three things you can share about yourself that someone might find interesting? How would it feel to have a give-and-take conversation?

During interactions with others, your physical symptoms of anxiety, like shaky hands or sweaty palms, might grab your attention and take it away from the other person because you are worried they will notice them. This can escalate your discomfort, causing you to excuse yourself prematurely (aka escaping). Has this ever happened to you? What if your symptoms went completely unnoticed by the other person? Describe how that interaction might have gone differently.

IMAGINE A SCENARIO

Use this visualization exercise to get in touch with what you might gain if you push through your anxiety.

1. Bring something to mind that matters to you but that you've avoided or neglected because of anxiety and fear. Picture the details. Paint the scene in your mind's eye.

2. Try to conjure what you would feel in your body if you approached what you are afraid of. Notice the physical cues. Can you feel your heart rate increase or your stomach sink? Remind yourself that you're safe; you're just pretending.

3. Imagine you follow through with whatever has been frightening you into inaction, and imagine how you would feel if you did that. What would you gain?

Think of an important situation you have been avoiding because it causes you anxiety. Briefly describe the situation using factual terms, such as "asking my boss for a raise":

Now, what four steps can you take to work up to that follow-through? Let's use a simple example:

- Step 1: "On Monday, think of my boss for three minutes and repeat to myself, *This person is safe.*"

- Step 2: "On Tuesday, make eye contact and say hello to my boss."

- Step 3: "On Wednesday, ask my boss a work-related question."

- Step 4: "On Thursday, ask my boss if we can schedule a time to talk next week."

- Goal: "Ask my boss for a raise."

Your steps will probably be more involved and may take more time. Create a four-step plan now to approach the situation you've been avoiding:

Goal:

Mindfulness brings me to the moment. The moment is the place I experience life at its fullest. I choose to live, not just exist.

A phobia is intense anxiety toward a particular experience—for example, encountering spiders or snakes or a fear of crowds or heights. Do you have any phobias? If so, how is this different from your usual anxiety? Describe what you think might happen if you encounter this situation. Are you willing to give yourself a chance to discover if what you fear will actually happen? If so, what might this look like? Who might you turn to for help dealing with this?

Over the long term, avoidance generates more anxiety. Keep in mind that the problem is not the anxiety itself but how you respond to it. Describe a situation you generally avoid. If you avoid that situation, what other situations might you also avoid in the future? For example, if you are too anxious to go to the lunchroom at work, might you also avoid the company picnic, business meetings, and conventions? What opportunities would you miss?

Describe a time when you had a hunch or gut feeling (in other words, your anxiety was telling you to be on alert) and it turned out you were right on target. What happened? What consequence did you likely avoid? For example, maybe you avoided a meeting with a person whom you found out later had bad intentions.

OPPOSITE ACTION

When the body feels a certain way (angry or timid, for instance), it responds by quickly communicating those feelings to the outside world. For example, anger might make a person grimace, bare their teeth, and ball up their fists. Feeling timid might make a person shrink away.

These strong moods may make you feel unsafe, causing the avoidance behavior you want to change. To get your mood under control so that you can move forward despite your anxiety, try doing the opposite action to short-circuit those strong mental networks.

1. Visualize yourself feeling anxious. See your facial expression and body posture in full detail.

2. Figure out the opposite of your expression and posture. For example, if you slouch, stand up straight and look forward; if you slouch or look away, take a small step forward or lean forward; if your eyes are narrow, open them wider; if you're frowning, draw your lips upward.

3. Think of a situation that typically causes you anxiety. Once you have it firmly in mind, slowly reposition your body into the opposite action. You can do this subtly when facing the situation in real time, as well.

Accepting Anxiety

"Not everything that is faced can be changed, but nothing can be changed until it is faced."

—James Baldwin

Acceptance can be the first step in dealing with anxiety. Acceptance is saying that, in this moment, this what my body is experiencing. We accept that it is here in reality. This doesn't mean that will be true in the *next* moment, but it is true in *this* moment. Rather than judging it or trying to make it go away, it simply is. Try to stay mindful whenever you exercise acceptance of anxiety or other moods.

As much as we may like to own a time machine, the truth is we can't change what happened in the past—only our perception of it. Think of something that happened in the past that you wish you could change. Knowing that it is unchangeable, how might the acceptance of what happened help you move forward?

Although it can be hard to accept painful emotions, the consequences that come from not doing so far outweigh the pain of facing whatever it is you're really feeling. Write down some examples in your life where your lack of acceptance of your feelings has only caused you more negative emotion. Has it increased your anxiety? Caused you to siphon off large amounts of emotional energy in vain? Blocked joy and contentment? As you reflect on these, be honest with yourself and acknowledge the main feeling you tend to avoid that brings the most consequences to you—sadness, anger, anxiety, guilt, shame, frustration, joy.

KNOW IT, SHOW IT, LIVE IT

Practicing mindfulness, which you can do anywhere at any time, generally involves three steps: know it, show it, and live it. Being aware of what is going on in the moment can give you clues to anxiety triggers that your brain may notice but you didn't (the color of a room or a spinning fan, for instance). When you are mindful of the moment, you can better assure yourself that you are safe and those things are harmless. The more often you do this, the better you will become at noticing and accepting what's going on around you.

1. Take a few deep breaths to center yourself and remind yourself that you can only truly do one thing at a time. Right now, you are breathing.

2. Now, simply observe the situation around you. Use all five senses to determine what is present in this moment. What do you hear? What do you smell? What do you taste, feel, and see? (Take a solid minute or longer to do this when you first get started practicing.)

3. Switch from knowing the situation to describing or showing it. In objective terms, describe to yourself what you sensed. Some examples might be: "The cup is round. It is smooth on this side and rough on the other. I'm in a room with six sides, four walls, a floor, and a ceiling. I smell nothing. I hear a whirring."

4. Now that you know reality right now, try to live within it by responding to things as they occur in reality—not based on what they should be. Live within it the way you might dance to a song. Even if a song is new to you, you can usually pick up the beat and move along in time with it.

Thank you for your contribution, brain. I'm focusing on this moment right now. I appreciate your showing me the past and potential future.

You've probably heard, "The present is called the present because it is a gift." It's only in the present moment that we can take action and make a change. The past is simply a chain of present moments that eventually became past memories. Describe how this idea makes you feel, and whatever comes up for you, practice accepting those feelings.

We always have three options in any situation: 1) do nothing, 2) change the situation, or 3) accept the situation. Describe three separate times when you chose one of these options with regard to your anxiety. What differences did you notice between all three?

I only have control of myself and my actions.
I accept that I have no control over others or
their actions.

Have you ever seen a hero in a movie encounter quicksand? Rather than struggle, the hero must lie back and spread out to avoid getting sucked in. What in your life would you consider "quicksand"? How has struggling affected the situation? What might be your personal version of lying back and spreading out instead?

Not all distractions are avoidance behaviors. Sometimes, distracting yourself can be a helpful diversion to give you a break until you are ready to try to face the anxiety again. What types of diversions work for you? Describe how they are different from avoidance.

Accepting anxiety doesn't mean you're allowing it to control you. Acceptance doesn't even mean you like what you're experiencing. If there's a particular situation you have been avoiding, maybe it *will* be something you don't enjoy. Accepting that it may be uncomfortable or scary can help you take the leap. Imagine the worst-case scenario and describe how you think you will feel in that situation. Then do it and come back to this entry. Did the worst-case scenario happen?

FINDING THE JUDGMENTS

Start becoming aware of the judgments in your thoughts, no matter how small. Judging something is the opposite of accepting it. Noticing the difference will help you start exercising acceptance more often.

1. Get an index card or similar-size paper and a pencil or pen. Split the index card into two columns. Label one column "evaluative" and the other "should." Keep it handy throughout the day.

2. Notice when you think or say words about a situation like "worst, worse, good, better, best." For example, "This could be going better." Give yourself a checkmark in the "evaluative" column when you think it and two checkmarks if you say it.

3. Notice when you think or say "should" or "shouldn't." For example, "I shouldn't be feeling this way." Give yourself a checkmark in the "should" column when you think it and two checkmarks if you say it.

4. At the end of the day, how many times did you judge something? How could these judgments be influencing you? How might evaluating and accepting something for what it is help you feel better?

Dwelling on past negative experiences can be a tough habit to break. Keeping a record of positive events each day can be useful in changing this habit. While accepting that everything may not have gone the way you had hoped, describe three or more positive experiences you had today. Is this something you might want to do daily? How might rereading these positive experiences at some future time help you?

If you feel regret, you may be judging yourself for going against one of your values. Values are the things that give our lives meaning—health, beauty, family, community, etc. For example, if you value truth, perhaps you regret telling a lie. When you accept that the past is what it is and nothing you can do will change it, you can learn from what happened and use it to inform your future choices. List some of your values. If you are struggling, do an internet search for "core values" and determine which ones you share. How might living true to your values benefit you?

"Life is a series of natural and spontaneous changes. Don't resist them; that only creates sorrow. Let reality be reality. Let things flow naturally forward in whatever way they like."

—Lao Tzu

Anxiety decreases the same way it increases—step by step and with repetition. Think about something you would absolutely do if not for your anxiety. Here's an example: "Going on a long road trip with good friends." What about the situation causes anxiety? Break down all the reasons. Here it might be "traffic," "being in a cramped space," "no access to a restroom," and "being away from home."

Now, create scenarios where you can practice experiencing each of those situations separately to increase your tolerance. For example, go out at rush hour close to home and sit in the daily traffic, watch a movie in a comfortable straight-back chair (which may be the same length of stretches between rest stops), notice how long you wait before you normally use the restroom while visualizing the car ride, and practice being away from home for a long weekend.

With repetition and your goal in mind, your tolerance for the discomfort associated with each anxiety trigger will gradually increase and you'll be better able to accept that although there will be some discomfort, a fun road trip is worth it.

What might happen if you exposed yourself to something you've been avoiding or escaping? Write a story about the worst-case scenario in full detail:

Now, write a story about the best-case scenario, where you manage your thoughts, feelings, and behaviors despite feeling anxious:

Focusing on the positive feelings of the best-case scenario will help you shift your focus away from avoidance and escape to acceptance and a fuller life experience.

III

thoughts

We adults often base our behaviors on our thoughts rather than on impulses. As we age, we generally learn to delay gratification, prevent impulsivity, and how to plan. So it's perfectly natural to think about the future and make predictions about what's to come. However, this natural process becomes an anxiety trigger when the forecast is often one of doom, disaster, or catastrophe.

The unknown doesn't have to trigger anxiety, nor does the past. In "Separating Thoughts from Reality," you'll explore the difference between thoughts and facts. Then, in "Rewriting Your Internal Narrative," you'll have a chance to look at your past, present, and future through a new lens.

Separating Thoughts from Reality

"If a problem is fixable, if a situation is such that you can do something about it, then there is no need to worry. If it's not fixable, then there is no help in worrying. There is no benefit in worrying whatsoever."

—The 14th Dalai Lama

Can a thought cause anxiety? Absolutely. What's more, because the thought uses our internal voice, it has an authority other inputs don't have. This is often why anxiety can so quickly spread beyond a single concern to our general outlook. It's important to remember that thoughts are not facts, and we shouldn't always believe what we think. The ability to separate our thoughts from what is actually happening or likely to happen is a powerful tool to counter anxiety.

When you begin teasing apart feelings and thoughts, it can be helpful to know that thoughts are often multiword phrases, whereas feelings are often a single word. Sometimes people tell me they felt "like crying" or "like I wanted to leave" a situation. These are great examples of thoughts. If someone tells me they felt "tired" or "anxious," these would be examples of feelings. It's perfectly fine to notice either the feeling or the thought first. Which do you notice first? Give some examples. Which feels more powerful to you?

Thoughts lead to feelings. Write down three thoughts and the feelings they caused in you. Note how strongly you felt each feeling on a 1–10 scale (1 being not strong at all and 10 being the strongest you've ever felt that feeling) and jot that number down beside the feeling.

When we are caught up in anxious thinking, our thoughts feel entirely real. In truth, the anxious mind isn't good at differentiating the real from the unreal. In cognitive behavioral therapy (CBT), these are called cognitive distortions. Here are some common biases that our minds are prone to and that intensify anxiety.

- **All-or-nothing thinking:** Things are all good or all bad; you are perfect or a failure.

- **Catastrophizing:** You look to the future with sweeping negativity and forecast disaster instead of more realistic possibilities.

- **Labeling:** Applying a fixed, global label on yourself or others without including any context. ("I'm a loser," "I'm bad," "I'm inadequate," "I'm a burden.")

- **"Shoulding" and "musting":** You have rigid expectations for how you should or must act, and when these unreasonable expectations aren't met, you forecast horrendous consequences.

Which of the distortions do you relate to the most? In what ways have you experienced them? How might they have stopped you from seeing the reality about yourself or a situation?

NAME THAT DISTORTION

In the previous prompt, you learned the CBT terms for distorted thinking. To make this more personal to you, give these distortions your own clever nicknames. Use the nicknames to remind yourself when your thoughts are distorting reality. Here are some ideas:

- All-or-nothing thinking might be "It's win or lose!"

- Catastrophizing might be "Expect the worst because it's around the corner!"

- Labeling might be "Slap a sticker on that!"

- "Shoulding" might be "It's my way or the highway!"

Using these examples, jot down a few alternate terms that you'll remember and perhaps can make you laugh to get better at recognizing when cognitive distortions are at play.

Sometimes the brain shows us past events to let us decide what we "should" or "shouldn't" have done. Do you ever "should" yourself? What past events does your brain tend to replay for you and how does it make you feel? To counter the second-guessing, choose one and jot down three positive things that occurred based on the course of action you did take.

CHALLENGING ALL-OR-NOTHING THINKING

The thinking brain seems to love all-or-nothing thinking. In reality, the world is rarely black or white; there are usually many more shades in between. This exercise can help you understand this better.

1. Bring to mind a worry for your future, such as "I'm going to lose my job because I'm really going to mess this up."

2. Draw a small dot in the left-hand side of the space provided on the next page and write the thought below it. Above the dot, write "worst-case scenario."

3. Think of the opposite of the thought (the best-case scenario). For the example given, perhaps this is "I'm going to get a promotion because I'm going to ace this."

4. Draw another dot on the right-hand side of the space on the next page. Write the opposite thought below the dot and "best-case scenario" above it.

5. Draw a line between these dots. Now, draw a point on the line right in the middle of the two points.

6. Now, write a thought above it that reflects both points A and B being true or both points A and B being false. For example, here we might write, "I'll do okay on the project and keep my present job." If you like, add in a reason, like, "because that is far more likely than either the best-case or worst-case scenario."

What If? was a comic book series by Marvel Comics that I loved as a kid. It explored how things might have gone differently in the Marvel Universe if certain historical events had happened differently. Do you have your own series of "what if" comics that play out in your mind? Describe some of them and how they affect you.

Often "what if?" scenarios end in something bad happening, like "What if I plant a tree here and then it falls on my house someday?" And, in the imagined scenario, it does. Some experts believe this kind of thinking helped us survive in prehistoric times, but these days, it can interfere with living life free of anxiety. Write down three of your top "what ifs?" and turn them into positive statements. For the tree example, perhaps you might say, "The tree will grow nicely in that spot and stay healthy and safe for many years to come."

"Stop thinking, and end your problems."

—Lao Tzu

Do you catastrophize, assuming the worst *will* happen? When you are caught in the quicksand of anxiety, thoughts of worry may seem acute and reasonable. Stress hormones are released, anxiety builds, and it becomes difficult to distinguish the probable from the possible. You can ease your anxiety by "decatastrophizing." Try this out: describe the absolute worst-case scenario that could come from a decision you make (for example, "If I choose the wrong job, my life will be horrible").

Now, assess how likely this scenario is to occur (for example, "Even if this job isn't everything I want, I'm 95 percent sure it won't be bad enough to make my entire life horrible").

Finally, think about how you'd handle it if it did happen (e.g., "If it turned out to be the wrong job for me, I'd start applying for other jobs or see if I could go back to my old job").

The brain may use repetitive thoughts to keep us in a state of being prepared to take action or to seek out safety. Is there a thought that regularly runs through your mind? What is it? How does it make you feel when you think it? Does thinking about it over and over again help you? If not, challenge the thought. Are any cognitive distortions present? If so, which one?

When it comes to thoughts, avoidance (which you learned is a symptom of anxiety) might sound like this: "I don't really want to go to work" or "All I want to do is go back to bed." What thoughts preceded those avoidance thoughts? Is there a meeting you're dreading? Deeply explore the reasons behind any thoughts that try to convince you *not* to go through with what you need or want to do.

Sometimes anxious thoughts can spread from one topic to others. For instance, if I worry about being robbed, later on I might start having anxiety about which streets I might be robbed on. Now, suddenly, I may start avoiding all streets, cars, or other things my mind wants to associate with it. Is there any thought that makes you anxious but you aren't sure why? How might it be connected to something else?

When trying to discern what is real, we often need to find what is fact and what is not fact. For instance, it is a fact that some of my hair is gray. The statement "Gray hair makes people look distinguished" is subjective and therefore not a fact. Think about a recent situation when a thought caused you discomfort. What was your thought at the time? Write down the facts of the situation as well as the subjective parts of the situation.

My thoughts just want to protect me. I cannot tell the future. I can only know what is happening right now in this moment.

Any thought that predicts a negative outcome can cause anxiety. Sometimes, it helps to compare the prediction with actual real-world events. For example, if I think, "My boss will yell at me if I tell him I didn't meet this week's quota," I might consider how many times the boss has actually yelled at me. If never, what are the real chances my boss will raise their voice to me? Try this with a situation where you are predicting that something negative will happen. Compare this to situations where the opposite occurred. Which seems more likely to happen?

READING MINDS

As much as we want to believe we can know what other people are thinking about us, we simply cannot read someone else's mind. Here's a fun way to debunk mind reading with a friend:

1. Think of an image or experience. Keep it in mind.

2. Ask your friend to guess what you are thinking. Don't give them any clues. If you are feeling generous, give them three chances. There's a good chance they will be totally or mostly off base.

3. Tell them what you were thinking, and switch roles. Let your friend think of something while you try to guess what it is. Chances are you were totally or mostly off base, too.

4. Ask yourself if you still believe that you can know what other people are thinking if they don't tell you.

When worrisome thoughts are troubling you, it's helpful to ask yourself if there is something you can do to ease your concern or if the situation just needs to play itself out. This is the difference between productive and unproductive worry. Worrying about a looming storm is unproductive unless it gets you to prepare for the bad weather in case it comes your way. Write down something you are worried about and explore if it is productive or unproductive.

Have you heard the term "self-fulfilling prophecy"? This is where we forecast an outcome and then advertently (or inadvertently) do things to increase the chances it will come true. Sometimes, the brain paralyzes us with thoughts, which, if we take no action, will increase the chances of the negative outcome. Have you made any self-fulfilling prophecies? How can you phrase things differently next time and take actions based on those thoughts to support yourself in a similar situation?

Core beliefs are your central thoughts about yourself. If someone's core belief is "I am bad," they may find themselves picking at their flaws in different areas of life to prove to themselves that they are in fact bad. They might have thoughts such as, "I'm a terrible employee," "I'm a bad parent," or "I'm a lousy spouse." Think about the negative things you say about yourself. Can you identify a core belief that draws them all together? Debunk the core belief by listing all evidence to the contrary.

My thoughts are separate from who I am.
I am so much more.

Rewriting Your Internal Narrative

"Each of us is a unique strand in the intricate web of life and here to make a contribution."

—Deepak Chopra

A discussion of thoughts would be incomplete without thoughts about yourself. If you're struggling with anxiety, your internal commentary may very well be overly critical and unkind. Negative thoughts that involve you, your nature, and/or your future can profoundly increase anxiety and, with repetition, can lead to depression. You *can* rewrite your internal narrative to put the past aside and bring you into your truth today.

"You catch more flies with honey than with vinegar," as the saying goes. Being kind to yourself can be more productive than being harsh. How might being kind to yourself in your thoughts help you "catch more flies"? Give yourself some compliments now.

Looking back at the previous prompts, what is one of your "vinegar" thoughts you say about yourself? Say it to yourself out loud. Now, imagine that you are saying it to a child. Would you still say it? Why or why not?

THOUGHT DIFFUSION

Thoughts only stick around if we continue to focus on them. Instead, let them naturally flow out of your mind with this exercise.

1. Find a comfortable position, take a few deep breaths to encourage relaxation, and imagine a blue sky.

2. As thoughts come to you, imagine they are written in puffy cloud letters across the sky.

3. Watch as the clouds dissolve or move out of your field of vision, as they are prone to do, and let them take your thought with them.

4. Do this for each thought that comes to you for five or so minutes.

Have you ever wondered how negative thoughts about yourself started? You don't have to know this to change them, but it can be helpful to put it in perspective. Think back. Do you remember the first time you heard that negative statement about you? Who said it? Where were you? How did it make you feel? Is it similar to how you feel today?

We tend to be our own worst critics. What is the most critical thing you've ever said about yourself? For example, someone might tell themselves that they are a horrible friend. What might they tell themselves instead? Maybe, "I'm working on being a better friend." Rephrase your worst critical comment about yourself with more self-compassion and self-acceptance.

I have always been, I am in this moment, and I will always be . . . worth it.

TRUST FALL

This activity presents the opportunity to rewrite some things you might be telling yourself about yourself.

You'll need:

- Pen

- Paper

- Two to three friends or loved ones

1. Ask two or three people to honestly share with you their thoughts and feelings about you on a sheet of paper.

2. What do you think they will write about you? Write your predictions—including anything negative that comes to mind—on another sheet of paper, but don't let them see it.

3. Later, when you're alone, compare the papers. Are you surprised? Were any of your predictions accurate?

Negative thoughts about oneself generally go in one of these categories: 1) "I'm bad, worthless, evil, useless . . ." 2) "I'm a failure, lazy, unmotivated, unworthy . . ." or 3) "I'm dumb, rejectable, abandonable . . ." Do any of your self-critical thoughts fall into these categories? What is the reverse of each of these thoughts? Jot down your self-critical thoughts and their reverse thoughts.

OPPOSITE DAY

When I was in grade school, Wednesday was the unofficial "opposite day." We could say something out of character and follow it up with "Wednesday is opposite day!" That would cause a chuckle and some mirth. Every day can be an opposite day for your mind.

1. Pick an anxiety-provoking thought. Here, we will use "I'm a failure."

2. Now, find the opposite affirming thought. "I'm *not* a failure" won't work since it still has "I'm a failure" in there. We have to find a way to say it in the affirmative, not the negative. In other words, it can't have "no," "not," "never," etc.

3. A possibility here might be, "I'm successful in many aspects of my life."

4. If the thought you chose is a common offender, then write this down and read it out loud when you need it.

If the brain quickly commits to a thought, that's evidence that it has had some practice and wants to take the path of least resistance. Altering this by uttering the opposite serves to help make the path harder for your brain while replacing it with something that serves you better.

Cycling the same thoughts over and over makes the brain feels like it is doing its job. What thoughts tend to go through your head repeatedly with regard to who you should or should not be? Do these thoughts help you take positive action? If not, how can you rephrase these repetitive thoughts to be more action-oriented?

Listen to your internal dialogue. What is its tone? Is it soothing or harsh? Practice speaking to yourself with a self-compassionate tone. For example, rather than passing harsh judgments such as, "You're so stupid!" you could instead gently say, "You failed that test, so you need to study harder or get extra help." Write a few self-compassionate statements here and practice saying them in your head.

It is easy to believe thoughts because they come from within. Write down one or two thoughts about yourself and consider if it's possible that these thoughts aren't true. List a few facts (objective observations) that prove what your brain is saying is false.

The key to rewriting your narrative is to develop a different way to view an event or situation. So, review the facts you gathered in the previous prompt. Do your original thoughts align with the facts? If not, rewrite each thought in a way that fits the facts—*even if you don't believe it at first.*

Think of a recent outcome of an event, situation, or experience that caused you to berate yourself. What is your inner critic saying about you? Gather facts to the contrary and view the situation in a new light. Rewrite the scenario from this more objective perspective.

Do certain tasks, hobbies, or people make you feel kinder to yourself? Is your internal voice less critical in these circumstances? If so, what and who are they? If not, what types of activities might you like to try and who would you like to spend time with to access more positive feelings about yourself?

"If we could change ourselves, the tendencies in the world would also change. As a man changes his own nature, so does the attitude of the world change towards him."

—Gandhi

If your negative thoughts about yourself make you want to avoid people because you fear they will see your flaws, you need to develop some counterthoughts. A counterthought must be resolute, one-directional, and prompt you to take action. For example, "I'm not good at small talk, and I'll feel left out of the conversation " is a negative thought; a counterthought might be, "I am a good listener. To feel included, I'll nod and smile to show I'm interested." List some negative thoughts and add the counterthoughts you might use in an anxiety-provoking situation.

CHANGING *BUTS* TO *ANDS*

The thinking brain loves binary options—off or on, up or down, bad or good, so on and so forth. This activity may help you find a place in which two things that seem opposite can actually be true at the same time.

1. Find a binary thought. For example, "I want to succeed, but this isn't working."

2. Now, replace the "but" with the word "and." This leaves us with "I want to succeed and this isn't working." Now, we still want to succeed and have the option of changing "this" into a path that might work better.

3. Whenever you are in a binary thought situation, try this word switch to see if it gives you clues on what could happen next.

Reflect on the writing you have done in this section. What positives came out of it? What new things did you learn about yourself? In a sentence or two, write a positive action statement that can guide your future moments.

My story is made up of ideas within chapters of books. I continue to write my story each day.

You have come a long way through this journal so far. By taking a deeper look at your feelings, thoughts, and behaviors, you've gained valuable insight. You have a toolbox of strategies and practices to help you manage anxiety when it arises. To experience the kind of calm and ease you want in life, it's important to keep using your tools and ask for support when you need it.

In "Building Your Support Network," you'll have an opportunity to explore your current relationships, cultivate new ones, and practice opening up to others. Then you'll learn how to build on the techniques you've learned and continue to use them into the future.

Building Your Support Network

"The world is so empty if one thinks only of mountains, rivers and cities; but to know someone who thinks and feels with us, and who, though distant, is close to us in spirit, this makes the earth for us an inhabited garden."

—Johann Wolfgang von Goethe

Evidence suggests that we are pack animals. Together, we truly are greater than the sum of our parts. We can share our challenges and help one another heal, as well as celebrate our successes and accomplishments. This sharing can help us reduce anxiety and stay diligent to limit anxiety in our daily lives.

I take action to give and receive
love unconditionally.

Sometimes it is helpful to take stock of our current relationships. Reflect for a moment on the relationships in your life and write them all down. Draw a small heart next to people to whom you feel close. Put a small star next to those you'd like to be closer to. How long have they been in your life? How or where did you meet them? What steps can you take to reach out?

AUTHENTICITY IN ACTION

Some people struggle with the idea that sharing their worries, fears, or anxiety might be perceived by others as weakness or worthlessness, or as failing to fulfill their role in the relationship. In fact, the opposite is true: revealing our feelings to a trusted partner or friend deepens our relationships.

1. What are some of your anxiety-causing situations, thoughts, or behaviors?

2. Name one to three people with whom you have a close relationship.

3. Think about what you will say to one of these people about your anxiety and write it down. For example, you might say, "I feel afraid when I have to stop suddenly while driving," or "I get worried when people raise their voices around me."

4. Now, actually say this to the person. How did they react? Has your relationship changed since sharing this? If you could do it over, would you tell them anything more or less?

PEOPLE FINDER

If you've been avoiding interacting with others because of your anxiety, you may be feeling lonely. With the insight you've been gathering and the strategies you've been practicing, it's time to find your people—like-minded people who you will enjoy being around.

1. Think about who you are and what you are about. Do you like to bake, sew, read, cosplay, or train animals?

2. Search for groups in your area with similar interests. You might use social media or community bulletin boards to find groups that appeal to you.

3. Do you have a community college or school near you? Take a look at their class offerings. Continuing your education in your interests is a great way to find like-minded people.

4. Would you like to add exercise to your socializing? Many organizations and clubs exist just to play organized sports or work out together.

5. If there's one thing communities always need more of, it's volunteers. Call or email local not-for-profit organizations that interest you to see if any volunteer opportunities exist.

6. Write down five groups that appeal to you. Contact each and record their next meeting times.

7. Pick one to attend this week, one for next week, and so on until you have one new group each week for the next five weeks.

8. Don't forget to plan travel arrangements if you need transportation or other assistance to get there on time.

Social media can help you find your people, and sometimes you can receive great support from your "friends" and followers. However, there's a downside: comparing yourself to others. Instead, remind yourself that social media profiles and posts are tiny snapshots of someone's life. What can you gain by focusing on and celebrating your own journey rather than getting caught up in theirs?

Sometimes we have needs and wants that are best met by another person. This is part of the human condition. What are your needs in a relationship? What do you want from your relationships?

We all know someone in life who has a "my way or the highway" attitude. This is someone who has to have their way regularly. Who is this in your life? Do you enjoy spending time with them? Has this person ever lost a relationship because someone got tired of their actions and took the "highway" instead?

I have wants and needs because
they are part of being human.

Giving too much as well as expecting too much in a relationship can be problematic. Unfortunately, when give and take get out of balance, the experience may be less than positive. Reflect on a time when you felt resentment or imbalance in a relationship. If you are still in this relationship, what steps can you take to find more balance?

It's hard for others to meet our needs or wants if they don't know what they are. Think about a time when you tried to express a need and the other person didn't meet it. How did you express it? Remember, others cannot read our minds. Write down three needs you have. Now, put them into this template: "I need/want you to give me [thing you need/want]. It will [thing that will change/get better] when you do." If it is a close relationship, you might want to add "Without it, I feel [how you feel]."

Saying no is often difficult because we want to be able to say yes; it feels less stressful to just give in. Sometimes, though, saying no is necessary. Think about past situations in which you wanted to say no but didn't. How did they turn out? What is someone currently asking of you that you'd like to refuse? After you've written out the request, write "No." Remember, no is a complete sentence; this is all you will need to say when the request is made again.

Sometimes we face special challenges in our lives that only those who have gone through it truly understand. A support group can be a powerful ally in your efforts toward anxiety relief. You can find both in-person and online support groups. How might someone who relates to what you've been through be a resource? What support group topics might be sources of comfort for you?

The Road Ahead

"My dear, life rarely gives us what we want at the moment we consider appropriate. Adventures do occur, but not punctually."

—E. M. Forster

As you move forward, it is important to value your progress rather than strive for perfection. Accept that there will be days when challenges arise. So too will there be days where you think, "Things are better and I don't need to worry about anxiety anymore." I wish my experience supported that, but it doesn't. To keep anxiety in a supporting role, you have to continue to actively care for yourself and prioritize living your life over giving in to the symptoms of anxiety.

Consider the possibility that when something doesn't go so well it can also be a victory. For instance, did you learn something from a poor outcome? If you know more now, doesn't that indicate you got something out of the experience—even if it wasn't what you initially wanted? Write about what you have learned from the challenges in your journey.

Getting an A+ on an exam makes us feel good, partly because someone agrees that our performance was perfect. If we continue to aim for this through life, we risk anxiety and the exhaustion that comes with it. Do you consider yourself a perfectionist? In what way? What would you need to know to realize that sometimes a lower grade is perfectly fine?

YOU WON BEFORE YOU STARTED

We often gauge victory by conditions being met or exceeding expectations. Ever wondered how much suffering this leads to? Let's find an alternative:

1. Reflect for a moment on how you came to be.

    - What are the chances you would be conceived, born, and come to this point in your life?

    - With all the elements in the universe, what are the chances that dust from stars would come together and form your physical being at this moment?

    - Is it possible that simply existing is remarkable? What does it mean that you have existed for every day of your life?

2. In truth, you were victorious over the odds before you were even born. You are a being composed of the dust from stars traversing the Earth.

3. Take this information and write an affirming statement about how you are already victorious.

The critical internal dialogue you have been learning to change may start up again if you find yourself struggling. Perhaps you missed an opportunity to practice a strategy, or maybe a coping skill is taking a little longer to develop. What kindness can you show yourself in the face of a mistake or a recurrence of your anxiety?

We may initially begin a new physical fitness routine to achieve a weight goal and then slack off a bit when we reach it. However, to maintain that goal, we must keep physically active. Strategies to ease anxiety are similar. Which activities from this book or elsewhere did you find particularly useful? Which would you like to try more often?

When I support myself right now,
I'm actively replacing "simply existing"
with "actively living."

Plan for a day when your anxiety pushes you to avoid everything by doing nothing. What is one thing you can do that will get you out of bed? What can you do next? And *then* what can you do?

Incorporating new practices can be easier if you know what to expect. Make a list of strategies to keep your anxiety-coping practice going. Each day, pick one thing and try to put it into action.

It's entirely possible that through your writing in this journal, you found something new that works for you. We must do what works. How did you figure it out? How did the new skill help you? When will you use it in the future?

TALK THERAPY GOALS

After all the work you've done in this journal, perhaps you have become interested in talk therapy. Talk therapy can be a powerful way to change how you think about things and make changes in life. Ask your doctor and trusted friends for recommendations, and see page 173 for resources. Before you contact any mental health professional, write down three things that you want to get out of therapy and ask the therapist about these as goals.

Goal 1:

Goal 2:

Goal 3:

_____

_____

_____

_____

Sometimes you may feel like you are in a losing battle with anxiety. Remember, anxiety exists for a reason: to keep you safe. It's not your enemy. It is just being overzealous. What can you tell yourself when your anxiety feels like the star in your film rather than a supporting actor? Come up with some affirmations you can tell yourself when you start feeling this way.

Some goals may sound a bit overwhelming and for good reason. For example, "I want to get fit" is actually a series of thousands of decisions. The goal "I want to cope with anxiety" is similar. But it doesn't have to overwhelm you if you just take one step at a time. Check in with yourself: What are you feeling and thinking? Do you feel anxious, worried, sad, nervous . . . ? What is one thing you can do in this moment to help yourself feel better without falling back on avoidance behaviors? Flip back through this journal and choose something if you need to.

If you continue to try just one skill or strategy at a time, you will remain aligned with your goal to experience more calm and ease. Committing to practice each day will keep you on the path toward developing a better relationship with your anxiety.

Every moment gives me a new opportunity to accept my life as it is rather than how I think it should be. I am exactly where I need to be.

Resources

Online

Acceptance and Commitment Therapy resources (PositivePsychology.com)

National Suicide Prevention Lifeline (1-800-273-8255)

Find a Therapist tool (PsychologyToday.com/us/therapists)

Further Reading

Be Calm: Proven Techniques to Stop Anxiety Now by Jill P. Weber. Emeryville: Althea Press, 2019.

Mind Over Mood: Change How You Feel by Changing The Way You Think by Dennis Greenberger and Christine A. Padesky. New York: The Guilford Press, 1995.

The Celestine Prophecy: An Adventure by James Redfield. New York: Warner Books, 1993.

Zen Mind, Beginner's Mind: Informal Talks on Zen Meditation and Practice by Shunryu Suzuki. Boulder: Shambhala, 2020.

References

Ackerman, Courtney. "How Does Acceptance And Commitment Therapy (ACT) Work?" December 14, 2020. PositivePsychology.com. PositivePsychology.com/act-acceptance -and-commitment-therapy/.

Afer, Publius Terentius. *Heautontimorumenos: The Self-Tormentor*. Project Gutenberg: Salt Lake City, 2007. Gutenberg.org/files/22188/22188-h/files/terence3_4.html.

Campolo, Bart. "605: Connection After Deconstruction." *Humanize Me*. Podcast audio, 56:45. BartCampolo.org/humanize-me-index.

Chopra, Deepak. "@deepakchopra: Each of us is a unique strand in the intricate web of life and here to make a contribution." July 13, 2014. Twitter.com/DeepakChopra/status /488350868949843968?s=20.

Dalai Lama, The. *The Dalai Lama, a Policy of Kindness: An Anthology of Writings by and About the Dalai Lama*. Edited by Sidney Piburn, Delhi: Motilal Banarsidass Publishers Private Limited, 2002.

Forster, E. M. *A Passage to India*. Project Gutenberg: Salt Lake City, 2020.

Gandhi, Mahatma. *The Collected Works of Mahatma Gandhi, Volume XII, April 1913 to December 1914*. Delhi-6: The Publications Division, Ministry of Information and Broadcasting, Government of India, 1964.

Goldsmith, H. H., Arnold Buss, Robert Plomin, Mary Klevjord Rothbart, Alexander Thomas, Stella Chess, Robert A. Hinde, and Robert B. McCall. "Roundtable: What Is Temperament? Four Approaches." *Child Development* 58, no. 2 (1987): 505–529.

Greenberger, Dennis, and Christine A. Padesky. *Mind Over Mood: Change How You Feel by Changing the Way You Think*. New York: The Guilford Press, 1995.

Kabat-Zinn, Jon. *Wherever You Go, There You Are: Mindfulness Meditation in Everyday Life.* New York: Hachette Books, 1994.

Kaur, Kawalpreet. *Depression Is Just a Word Unless It Happens to You.* Darshanpurwa: PustakRatna Prakashan, 2020.

Keller, Helen. *Let Us Have Faith.* New York: Doubleday, Doran & Co., Inc., 1940.

Levine, Peter, and Phillips, Maggie. *Freedom from Pain: Discover Your Body's Power to Overcome Physical Pain.* Boulder: Sounds True, Inc., 2012.

Linehan, Marsha. *DBT Skills Training Manual.* New York: The Guilford Press, 2014.

McKay, Matthew, Jeffrey C. Wood, and Jeffrey Brantley. *The Dialectical Behavior Therapy Skills Workbook: Practical DBT Exercises for Learning Mindfulness, Interpersonal Effectiveness, Emotional Regulation & Distress Tolerance.* Oakland: New Harbinger Publications, Inc., 2007.

Ratey, John J., and Richard Manning. *Go Wild: Eat Fat, Run Free, Be Social, and Follow Evolution's Other Rules for Total Health and Well-being.* New York: Little, Brown Spark, 2014.

Thuret, Sandrine. "You Can Grow New Brain Cells. Here's How." TED@BCG London, 2015. TED Talk.

Tzu, Lao. *Tao Te Ching.* Translated by Stephen Mitchell. New York: HarperCollins Publishers, 2006.

van der Kolk, Bessel. *The Body Keeps the Score: Brain, Mind, and Body in the Healing of Trauma.* New York: Penguin Books, 2015.

Weber, Jill P. *Be Calm.* Emeryville: Althea Press, 2019.

Youssef, Nagy A., Laura Lockwood, Shaoyong Su, Guang Hao, and Bart P. F. Rutten. "The Effects of Trauma, with or without PTSD, on the Transgenerational DNA Methylation Alterations in Human Offsprings." *Brain Sciences* 8, no. 5 (2018): 83. doi.org/10.3390/brainsci8050083.

Acknowledgments

This writing would not have been possible without the years I spent with my clinical supervisors and colleagues over the years. Thank you to all of the professionals at Callisto Media, especially my editors, Adrian Potts and Carol Rosenberg, for their patience and kind guidance, as well as Ashley Popp for bringing this project to my attention. I extend enormous gratitude to my wife and children, who were patient with me while I wrote.

Lastly, I want to thank the hundreds of people I've had the privilege of serving over the years. Without your kindness, vulnerability, and resilience, I would not be able to connect or affect the changes that bring relief to so many.

I am humbled to serve from the shoulders of giants.

About the Author

Christopher C. Hutcheson is an award-winning clinical social worker and author. His private practice, Gentle Beacon, specializes in the treatment of anxiety and depression in Lafayette, Indiana. He believes that innovating new ways to connect (like this book) will lead to healing in individuals, communities, and our world. Keep up with Christopher at GentleBeacon.com, or, if you'd like to connect with Christopher, send him an email at chris@gentlebeacon.com.

CPSIA information can be obtained
at www.ICGtesting.com
Printed in the USA
BVHW090058091021
618439BV00001B/2

9 781638 070115